C#
Object Oriented Programming
and
.NET Framework

SRIDHAR CHENOOR

ISBN 979-8-89475-603-5

Sri Ganapati, Srinivasa Govinda, Sri Guru Rayaru, Sai Swami.

With the blessings of **Maa Saraswati, Vidya-Buddhi Pradayini** (Goddess of all learning), my parents, all family, including my academic teachers and students, who have made this possible. And, of course my sincere thanks to **Microsoft .NET,** the beautiful **C# language** and all those who contributed to it.

ॐ पूर्णमदः पूर्णमिदं पूर्णात्पुर्णमुदच्यते
पूर्णश्य पूर्णमादाय पूर्णमेवावशिष्यते॥
ॐ शान्तिः शान्तिः शान्तिः॥

"What is visible is the infinite. What is invisible is also the infinite. Out of the Infinite Being the finite has come, yet being infinite, only infinite remains."

"Om Peace, Peace, Peace"

Contents

Contents

Please make a note that all code examples and program code in the book have been developed in Visual Studio 2022 community edition. So you can install one on your system to go Hands On and Try code examples on your system.

Prologue

Origins of the Object Oriented Programming Methodology:

The PC world in the 1980s underwent significant changes, with superior hardware capabilities in very fast processors and high-capacity memory (both primary and secondary storage) devices, along with the PC availability at very affordable prices.

This change led to the possibilities of developing complex application software. And although this meant complex applications could be developed, it involved reasonably long efforts in software analysis and design. The programming methodologies prevalent at the time, quite didn't aid in a seamless manner, software development and its maintenance (i.e. need to affect modifications to a software, called versioning) typical to software development business. Some modifications meant, addressing the entire application program parts. That was quite tedious. Not just tedious, but the implications were serious cost and time overruns of the software projects, proving a nightmare to the programming community.

Exactly at this time, when the programmer and software developer community was faced with this critical situation, that, Object Oriented Programming (**OOP) methodology emerged, and came as a boon to software developers in not only reducing tedious and time-consuming programming efforts, but also contributing to manifold reduction in the costs of software development and its maintenance, that the developer community delighted in.**

Internet and the origins of the Microsoft .NET Framework:

Internet growth in the late 90s was a major force influencing the society, so much so that all the businesses began to go for web-based implementations of their existing applications to meet the wider internet audience demands. Inevitably, Microsoft realized that the DNA architecture (in vogue then) implemented by the COM/DCOM technologies that supported internet-based applications development were inadequate (for it complicated things with disparate technologies and laborious tasks). However, the fact that Internet and web protocol standards are platform neutral compelled Microsoft to redesign the existing developer tools and technologies (COM/DCOM) to adapt with internet and web standards naturally. Also, the target in mind was a **whole new execution environment** (an intelligent one at that, including new generation runtime features such as garbage collection, type safety checking, security...), while addressing the drawbacks in COM/DCOM. **The final outcome was the .NET framework.**

The .NET Framework is **fully 'Object Oriented Programming' based** and essentially **consists of a gigantic set of built-in classes** (in the form of libraries referred to as Framework Class Library - FCL) readily available for use in applications, and an **intelligent execution environment** called **Common Language Runtime (CLR).**

At the core of all .NET application development is this Framework, that is, without the .NET Framework, no .NET application is possible.

To surmise, the key goals in designing the .NET Framework were

(a) **to provide a basic infrastructure for application programming with methods that are consistent across different types of applications** (be it windows or internet-based web applications, so on.), **and languages**.

(b) In the internet world, if distributed computing is the norm, then **the divided application parts should be able to interface or communicate seamlessly, irrespective of the environments they live in.** This concept basically implies **achieving an application that is not tied to any specific platform**, in turn meaning, having a development environment that goes with open internet/web-based standards. Precisely what the .NET Framework embraces.

This book focuses mainly on **part (a)** mentioned above, and does not deal with part (b).

C# and Object Oriented Programming:

The art of object-oriented programming, with above mentioned features, can well be realized through **C#**. C# (pronounced c-sharp) is a **simple yet powerful, modern, 21st century object-oriented programming language developed by Microsoft.**

Appreciable unique features of C# are Delegates, Attributes based dynamic programming, Indexers, Generics as understood by C# that are not found in other object-oriented programming languages.

Typical structure of a C# program:

```
using System;
namespace Container
{
class Program
{
public static void Main()
{
Console.WriteLine("Hi! World");
}
}
}
```

CHAPTER ONE

Introduction to Basic Types, Operators and Program Flow Control Statements

To be able to write meaningful computer programs (applications), it takes appreciating and developing some level of skills in the Art of Programming.

Writing programs involves understanding how programs are written and constructed in terms of basic building blocks of a program - items (program variables, operators), code blocks, (program flow control statements – selection-based, repetition-based statements – and also method definitions), that makeup a class definition, and such. These constitute the basic building blocks of a program structure. This section is aimed at appreciating this programming art.

To start with let's get to some definitions:

Data: A value that is of value. It is a value that represents any fact around us. It is an object attribute's value. For a clear understanding, it is illustrated in the following example.

Let us consider a Person object, then the typical attributes or properties of the person object, would be

Name (person's name) and person's Age. So, name and age values of a person are data.

Data type: The type of data or value in question. e.g. the value 10, a number is seen as integer type, "John" - name of a person is seen as string type. So, we may define a string as a sequence of characters as in the value "John".

Also make a note that, when it comes to C# or .NET, we rather see every datatype also, as an object type.

Refer to Appendix A to get a clear understanding of Object type.

Variable: A program item that stores data or value. As the name suggests, the object data/value it stores can be varying or changing. At one point of execution, it can be storing one value, and at another point assigned a different value, so on.

We can see a variable name (identifier) as a name given to a location/block in memory where it stores a value or object. In other words, a location/block in memory got identified with a name using which we can access the value/object stored in there.

Constant: A constant is contrary to a variable. A constant is unchanging, invariable and fixed. Example Mathematical constant PI (22/7).

Variable and Variable Type

When we work with variables in a program, we should have knowledge of the **type of data or object** a variable would store.

Code Example:

```
int x;
float y;
```

So, in the preceding code lines we see, x is a variable declared as integer type. That means it will store integer values. Similarly, y is declared as a floating-point type, and stores floating-point values.

Predefined basic built-in types of C#

A type in C# (.NET) is either a value type or a reference type.

The distinction between these two is that value type data (objects) are allocated memory on a stack structure whereas reference types are allocated memory on a heap (a managed heap). And value type variables directly store value or object, but in the case of reference type variables, we can say there is a level of indirection because they do not store value or object directly, but do so indirectly (as they store a reference to objects). Because of this, when we assign a data/object stored in a value type variable to another, then a copy of the data/ object is assigned and stored.

Also, value type and reference type variables differ in how and when the objects they store are deleted from memory after they have gone out of scope.

A value type object on stack is removed soon its lifetime gets over as it goes out of scope, whereas reference type object is removed by Garbage Collector. A Garbage Collector is a program built into the Common Language Runtime (CLR), that manages the object disposal and cleanup job. Garbage Collector program is designed, based on an algorithm that determines when exactly an object would be garbage collected, after it has been marked as garbage. As we cannot know when exactly the object will be disposed, it is referred to as indeterministic finalization.

So, because of the garbage collection feature, a programmer in .NET environment can be relieved of the burden of the memory management task. This is auto-memory management.

More about it in the GC section.

So let us look at some basic types that C# (.NET) provides.

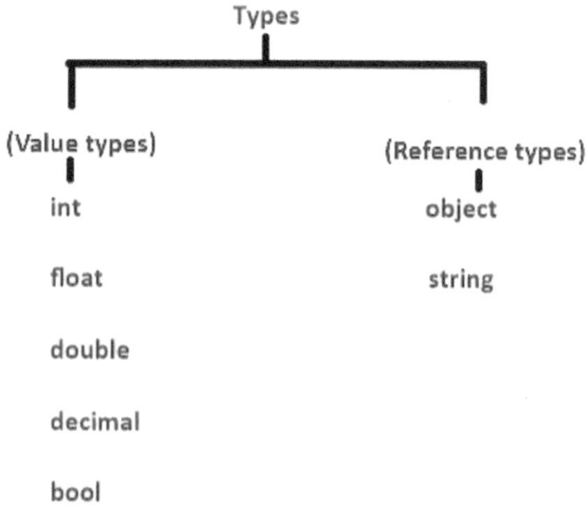

Built-in basic data types

Below is the list of some of the notable C# types that map to their corresponding .NET types

C# Types	.NET System Types
int	System.Int32
float	System.Single
double	System.Double
decimal	System.Decimal
bool	System.Boolean
char	System.Char
string	System.String
object	System.Object

C# (**type** keywords) mapping to .NET System types

So now, let's see and begin to get some ideas of how to work with these datatypes and variables.

```
int x = 100;
```

So, in the above code line statement, what we have done is we have declared a variable x of integer data type and then assigned it the value 100.

Now the value 100 is an integer and so it makes proper sense because the variable x has been declared to be integer type, so, an integer value got assigned to it.

Also, the above code line can be split into two lines as follows, and produce the same effect.

```
int x;
x = 100;
```

In real-time, for the most part that is how it would be, we just declare a variable, that's it. Later at some other line in execution, a value would be assigned to it.

Literals

The value **100** is a **literal**. Similarly, the value 23.24 is another literal value but, it is considered a floating-point value. So, from this we should infer that **even literals carry type meaning** and are seen to be of specific type based on the literal value's form or expression format.

```
float f = 23.12;
```

In the above code line, f is a variable declared to be floating-point type. The value being assigned goes with the type because 23.12 is seen a floating-point value.

```
decimal val = 122.44M;
```

Notice in the preceding code line the use of the suffix M. If we do not add that suffix then the literal value would be regarded a float value, so we need to explicitly convert it to decimal type value, by using the suffix 'M'.

Note:- uint, short, long types are **variants of int.** But they differ in the range of integer values they support.

Types float, double and **decimal;** these although represent floating point type values they differ in their size and precision levels.

Size of **float** type is **32-bits** whereas the size of **double** type is **64 bits;** double type has been named so because its size is double that of float and provides a higher precision level compared to float type. Also **float** type values are subject to rounding errors that might prove to be significant in some calculations. Double type is generally used for real values except financial calculations that demand high accuracy.

Size of **decimal** type is **128-bits,** and precision level is very high when compared to **float** and **double types,** and therefore it is used in financial calculations (in accounting, stocks, trading..) where a infinitesimally small fractional value can make a significant difference and impact

Default values of variables

Default value is the value stored in a variable by default when we do not initialize or explicitly assign it a value.

default value for int type is 0; default value for float type is 0.0f; default value for double type is 0.0d; default value for decimal type is 0.0m; default value for bool type is false; default value for char type is '\0'; default value for string type is null; default value for object type is null.

These default values apply only to variables declared as fields at the class level.

Please note that these default values do not apply to a variable declared inside a method. We shall look at and understand variable declaration in a method in the next chapter in Methods section.

Nullable types

Note that we can assign a *null* value to value types such as int, float, only when they are declared as nullable.

*So, if we should enable assignment of a **null** value to an int type variable, then we should explicitly declare it as nullable using '?' (symbol for nullable operator)*

example:

```
int? x = null; //is ok, because x (int
type) got declared as nullable using
'?' operator
```

Inferred or implicitly typed variable:

```
var x = 100; //x here is integer type
var s= "joyful"; // s here is string type
```

Comments

A comment is **a non-executable line(s)** of text, which serves as documentation that describes in brief, the purpose of a code item or code block in a program. Single line comment is declared using '//' and multi-line comment is declared using '/*' to indicate the begin of comment block and '*/' to indicate the end of comment block.

Identifiers

An identifier is a name given to a program item such as a variable or a method or a type.

Identifiers can begin with an underline or any Unicode character that is allowed. Keywords are not allowed and also identifier cannot contain formatting Unicode characters.

While choosing an identifier name, see that it is appropriate to the context. It also enhances readability and follows a standard convention and suggested good coding practices.

Operators:

An operator is a symbol or symbols that stands for a specific operation with regard to its operand types.

They can be grouped into various groups based on their functionality and associated operand(s).

Listed below are some operators:

Arithmetic operators

+, -, *, /, %

Relational operators

>, <, >=, <=, !=, ==

Logical operators

&&, ||, !

Program: A series of instructions that represents and performs a specified application task. They are executed in top-down linear flow structure.

Any meaningful instruction given in a language is made up of parts of speech of the language in some order or combination, as defined by and in conformity with the grammar (syntax) rules of the language. Thus, it makes meaningful communication possible for a program instruction to be carried out successfully.

In other words, it is words that are arranged in some structures such that they communicate or convey intended meaning.

Note: Writing instructions in a specific chosen language is called coding.

So coding is nothing but the act of writing program instructions in a chosen language for implementation.

A look at Console class

Console class is present in the System namespace.

When we work with program editors such as Visual Studio, for writing programs, Visual Studio will automatically add references to a few base libraries and also import a set of standard namespaces by default in the code files, thereby reduce the programmer's effort, in doing that. If the programmer is using a raw text editor such as a Notepad to write programs, then programmer will have to explicitly import, the required namespaces by writing *using* statements. So, to access the Console class without typing System.Console each and everytime we use it, all we have to do is, make sure that there is this **using System;** statement at the top, in the code file in which we use Console class. Thereafter we can simply refer to Console class just by typing **Console**.

Coming to the Console class. The Console class represents streams of the standard Input/Output console, that is, the standard input console is the keyboard and the standard output console is the screen or the monitor.

So, when we should accept inputs into a program or, write or display some output on to the screen we use the Console class.

The most frequently used methods of the Console class, that help us in this regard are WriteLine(), for writing output text on to the screen, and ReadLine() for accepting input from the user through the keyboard.

The following are a few examples of its usage

```
Console.WriteLine("Hello World");
int x = int.Parse(Console.ReadLine());
Console.WriteLine(x);
```

Program Flow Control Statements

Selection based (branching statements):

The **if** statements are branching type statements, therefore we use them, **when we should choose one**

block of code over other blocks, that form a logical group of code blocks that are grouped, based on the evaluation of conditional expression for execution. Sometimes we simply use if statement to decide whether to execute a block of code or not. The following example illustrates the logically grouped code blocks of an if statement:

if statement

```
if (boolean condition) [{] statements
[}]
[else if (boolean condition) [{]
statements [}]]
[else[{] statements [}]]
```

Example code snippet:

```
  int m1 = 54, m2 = 43, m3 = 72, m4 =
  84, m5 = 60;
float average = (m1 + m2 + m3 + m4 +
m5) / 5;
  if (m1 > 40 && m2 > 40 && m3 > 40 &&
  m4 > 40 && m5 > 40 && average > 80)
Console.WriteLine("Result Grade - A+");
  else if (m1 > 40 && m2 > 40 && m3 > 40
  && m4 > 40 && m5 > 40 && average > 70)
Console.WriteLine("Result Grade - A");
  else if (m1 > 40 && m2 > 40 && m3 > 40
  && m4 > 40 && m5 > 40 && average > 60)
```

```
Console.WriteLine("Result Grade - B+");
  else if (m1 > 40 && m2 > 40 && m3 > 40
  && m4 > 40 && m5 > 40 && average > 50)
Console.WriteLine("Result Grade - B");
  else if (m1 > 40 && m2 > 40 && m3 > 40
  && m4 > 40 && m5 > 40 )
Console.WriteLine("Result Grade - C");
  else
Console.WriteLine("Not passed - Retry");
```

switch statement

```
switch (integral, enum, or string) {
case constant 1: statements...
case constant n: statements
default: statements
```

Switch *statement is another selection-based branching type statement. Following example illustrates the use of Switch statement*

Example code snippet:

```
    public enum DesignationGroup {
    Manager, Executive, Assistant }
    DesignationGroup desiGroup =
    DesignationGroup.Manager;
    switch (desiGroup)
{
case (DesignationGroup.Manager):
Console.WriteLine("Manager:Manage and
administer a group of people ");
```

```
break;
case (DesignationGroup.Executive):
Console.WriteLine("Executive:Execute
assigned task, report to a manager ");
break;
case (DesignationGroup.Assistant):
Console.WriteLine("Assistant:Assist
executive and manager in tasks, report
to executive ");
break;
default:
Console.WriteLine("Nothing");
break;
    }
```

Iteration based (looping statements)

Iteration based control is about repeatedly executing a block of statement(s) a specified number of times or until certain condition holds true.

The **for, foreach, while** statements enable us accomplish iteration control. These are also referred to as looping statements as they repeatedly loop a block of code.

For **loop**

```
for (
[initializer list];
[boolean condition];
[post-operation list]) {statements}
```

```
Example code snippet:
string str = "*#$@!%&";
for (int i = 0; i < str.Length; i++)
{
Console.WriteLine($"Ascii value of char
{str[i]} is {(int)str[i]}");
}
```

foreach loop

```
foreach (type id in collection)
{statements}
Code snippet:
foreach (char c in str)
Console.WriteLine($"Ascii value of char
{c} is {(int)c}");
```

while loop

```
while (boolean condition) {statements}

Example code snippet:
string str = "*#$@!%&";
int idx = 0;
while (idx < str.Length)
{

Console.WriteLine($"Ascii value of char
{str[idx]} is {(int)str[idx]}");
```

```
idx++;
}
```

do loop

```
do {statements}
while (boolean condition)
Example code snippet:
string str = "*#$@!%&";
int idx = 0;
do
{


Console.WriteLine($"Ascii value of char
{str[idx]} is {(int)str[idx]}");
idx++;
}while (idx < str.Length)
```

Suggested exercises for this chapter in further reading

1. Spend time in exploring all the basic (simple)
    types of C# (i.e. .NET). Grasp the knowledge of the
    sizes of these basic types and the range of values
    they support.
    (Hint: uint, long, short, float, byte, char.. their sizes
    and the range of values they support.)
2. Expand on the knowledge of the operators;
    get hold of a chart that shows all the possible
    predefined operators grouped by category
    (Arithmetic, Relational, Assignment, Bitwise
    operators..)

Study and gain knowledge of the precedence level of different operators in a chart or table form and the order of evaluation, when in a compound expression there exist operators of equal precedence.

Example: 10 + 2 * 22 / 4 or in variables expression form such as (x + y * z / d)

3. Expand knowledge on these possibilities of a mixed type expression involving values of different types, and the type of the resulting value. Example: 2 * 4.02

4. Understanding implicit (automatic) and explicit conversions and their implication in loss of value if any in an assignment operation. Define in your own words, What is meant by compatible and incompatible types with regard to type conversions?

5. Explore further how this knowledge of Types, in essence .NET types contributes to Common Language Specification (CLS) defined in the .NET Framework. What is the role of Intermediate Language (IL) code?

6. Conduct little research in understanding Parse function supported by the types.

7. Study and understand the role of the keywords 'skip', 'continue' and 'yield' with regard to looping statements.

CHAPTER TWO

Object Oriented Programming and C#

The features fundamental to object-oriented programming are **Encapsulation**, **Abstraction**, **Inheritance** and **Polymorphism**. The following are brief definitions of these features:

A class is a template or blueprint for a group of similar objects. And the creation of a class instance (in memory to hold object data) is referred to as an object. So, an object is an instance of a class.

A class definition essentially, is **Encapsulation** of code that represents related data members and methods (functions or operations) of an object it models, into a single unit.

Abstraction is this ability to hide, typically a class's method member implementations by way of encapsulation, and letting access to the method members to the external world (outside of a class) for their invocation by declaring the method members as public using public access modifier. Therefore, a public method member of a class is an interface (a connection point), to the external world (and is referred to as a secondary object interface). Also, without any mistake, abstraction means studying an object and stating its characteristics and properties, from points of view of solving the application problem on hand, as it is not possible to study any object fully, in its entirety.

The encapsulation feature of object-oriented programming, gives the programming world the advantage of being able to manage the programming task, in terms of smaller units of program code, called **objects**.

Further, it even gives the ability to extend the features of an existing pre-defined object, in a new object being defined. This act of extending, in OOP is called **Inheritance**. The most useful result of inheritance is code reusability, besides providing the ability to structure related objects in a hierarchy, also called object model.

Another very useful feature of OOP that simplifies programming efforts is that of polymorphism. **Polymorphism** means a single operation having multiple implementations.

Object Oriented Programming (OOP) - Overview

First, let's begin to understand and define what an **object** means. An **object** is a thing and seen to consist of properties, physical or imaginary, that are unique to the object type. As application developers or programmers, our true concern is to study and comprehend objects that define, and play a role in, the application (being defined). Chiefly we are interested in its attributes or properties, and its behaviour. Understanding **Behaviour of an Object**, is kind of asking: what does the object do? In other words, Behaviour, defines operation(s) an object supports in an application.

Being in the context, we now rather **see an application consist of, a set of objects that are related and connected in ways such that, the application is useful, in that it supports and performs operations expected from it**. And every application is defined in terms of the *features and functions* (or operations) it performs.

With the background we just had, we wish to conclude that building any application (software/program) is really a matter of defining software models (referred to as classes in OOP jargon) of constituent objects that makeup the application. Thus, we would do well, begin understand the concept of a Class.

From a **programmer's perspective** any type (class) that is defined and used in an application program is a software model/blueprint of an object, that belongs to application's business domain for which we are writing the application software.

* * * * *

C# Programming - > .Net Concepts

C# is a programming language built into the .NET Framework. Obviously at the core of C# is the .NET Framework. Therefore, it shouldn't come as a surprise but all the more justified that **the Type System specification defined by the framework is what C# has to comply with and implement. A discussion of C# types implicitly refers to the core .NET Type System**

Type

A type in C# (.NET) invariably means type of object. Makes complete sense as .Net Framework is fully object oriented and going by the point made in the previous paragraph, logically, C# too is fully object oriented.

C# provides a set of constructs (class, struct, enum, delegate, interface) that allow define/create new types (in essence classes).

A new type called **user-defined type or custom type** can be defined, using the above constructs. Types defined using struct, enum definitions result in value types. Whereas Types defined using class, interface, delegate definitions result in reference types.

Namespace:

The concept of Namespace is to group Types/Classes into logical containers. When an application program is of some size and order, then obviously the number of classes part of the application program grow to a point where, handling or managing them all, proves to be cumbersome and adds to confusion. In such a situation, one can organize these Types into different groups based on their characteristics and functionality **using the concept of Namespaces.**

Visualize a namespace as a logical container for a group of related classes or types.

example:

```
namespace AbcCompany.HR
{
class Employee
{
//Code
}
}
```

Note that the above definition is the same as:

```
namespace AbcCompany
{
    namespace HR
    {
        class Employee
        {
            //Code
        }
    }
}
```

Also, as a nice side-effect, the concept of namespace helps avoid name collision issues. It helps address conflicting situations arising out of two or more classes having the same name in the same application, albeit with different implementation purpose and meaning. We can address such naming conflicts or collision issues easily, by having these classes contained in different namespaces.

Key Note: A fully qualified name of a class even includes the namespace name. As in the above code example, to refer Employee class using its fully qualified name, we would do so with the following code line using the dot operator syntax.

```
AbcCompany.HR.Employee
```

So, for accessing the Employee class by code outside the namespace it is contained in, we need to do so using above code line, explicitly. Assuming we have to do it several times in the program, it will be tedious. So luckily, we have a short cut method.

We write a *using* statement at the top of the code file in which we should access Employee class and thereby avoid writing fully qualified name explicitly.

After writing the using statement, we can now access Employee class just by writing Employee, that's it.

```
Code:
using AbcCompany.HR;
```

It is simpler now and a great time saver. Right?

Important Note: Our main case study, for the discussions and code examples that follow, is an organization's typical Human Resources (HR) domain. Therefore, this and the following chapters address the Person, Employee, Full-time Employee, Part-time Employee objects of the domain. We address them only partially though, and not to be seen as part of a full-blown HR application. But the concepts help you build such applications, using the knowledge gained in the discussions, as most of it, serves object modelling knowledge that can be carried into designing such applications.

Encapsulation and Abstraction

Concept of Class

A class is a software model (a blueprint or template) of a group of similar objects.

Abstraction - when we study objects of a business application domain and design software model representations of the objects, we focus on, only the object details that are essential, from the application problem point of view and ignore or leave out other details. This act is referred to as abstraction.

Encapsulation - The very act of defining a class is the act of encapsulating or putting a wrapper around related data members and methods of a class. This is encapsulation.

Code example:

```
class Employee
{

public Employee()
{
this.Id = "Not set";
this.Name = "Not set";


}
public Employee(string Id, string Name)
{
this.Id = Id;
this.Name = Name;
    }
public void ShowPersonDetails()
{
Console.WriteLine("Emp Id:" + Id);
Console.WriteLine("Emp Name:" + Name);
}
    public string Id { get; set; }
public string Name{ get; set; }
}
```

Understanding *this* keyword:

In the constructor definitions code above, we find the use of *this* keyword. The, *this* keyword refers to the **object instance** on which the constructor method got invoked. We shall look at object instances a bit later in the **Objects** section that follows. Well now, on a closer look at the code, we see that the parameter names of the parameterized Employee constructor, and the instance variables (or fields) Id and Name of the class are identical, thus not using *this* keyword would result in a conflict. Clearly, in such a situation, *this* keyword comes to our rescue.

Also, for us this being the first instance of the use of *this* keyword in the program, it should add to our clarity in understanding the purpose and role of *this*.

Note: The **'this'** *keyword can only be used with* **instance members** *and* **it cannot be used** *with* **static members***, or in a* **static method or class***.* **The only exception to this rule you may say is when you define an Extension Method, and there too, it may appear just as a specifier for, the first parameter which is declared to identify the class the extension method extends or attaches to.**

```csharp
class Employee
{
    public Employee()
    {
        this.Id = "Not set";
        this.Name = "Not set";

    }
    public Employee(string Id, string Name)
    {
        this.Id = Id;
        this.Name = Name;

    }
    public void ShowPersonDetails()
    {
        Console.WriteLine("Emp Id:" + Id);
        Console.WriteLine("Emp Name:" + Name);
    }

    public string Id { get; set; }
    public string Name{ get; set; }
}
```

Class definition code

Objects (object instances)

Having defined Employee class, we can now create instances of the Employee class, referred to as **objects** in OOP terminology.

The code for creating an instance of a class is shown below:

```
Employee emp = new Employee();
```

```csharp
1   using System;
2   using System.Collections.Generic;
3   using System.Linq;
4   using System.Text;
5   using System.Threading.Tasks;
6
7   namespace InterfacesAndClasses
8   {
9       internal class EmployeeClassClientCode
10      {
11
12          static void Main()
13          {
14              Employee emp = new Employee();
15              emp.Id = "Emp2002_12";
16              emp.Name = "Suresh";
17              if (emp.Id == "Not set" && emp.Name == "Not set")
18                  Console.WriteLine("Set values for emp, Id and Name properties");
19              else
20                  emp.ShowPersonDetails();
21
22              Console.ReadLine();
23          }
24      }
25  }
26
```

Client program code that uses Employee class

We should understand that **emp** in the above code line is an object variable of type Employee, that holds a reference to a new Employee object instance that got created. The term **reference** simply means the base address of the memory space or location where the object resides.

To understand what is going on clearly, we can split the above code line into two statements and end up producing the same result.

We do that in the following two lines.

```
Employee emp;
```

```
emp = new Employee();
```

Having done what we wished for, let us now examine each of these lines and have a clear grasp of what each line does.

The code line statement -

```
Employee emp;
```

means emp is an object variable of type Employee.

*C# being a **strongly typed language**, when we should declare a variable, we should declare ahead (either explicitly or implicitly) the object type of the variable, in its declaration line itself, unlike weakly typed languages such as Javascript, that allow for declaration of a variable without specifying its type.*

Strongly typed languages contribute to a type-safe environment in which, type mis-match errors are virtually non-existent.

Next, the code line statement -

```
emp = new Employee();
```

means that **a new object instance of Employee type be created**, by invoking the default zero parameter constructor method. The parenthesis '()' is used **to specify** parameters i.e. **parameter list if any, that matches with the signature of the constructor that we wish to invoke.** If we wish to invoke 'zero parameter constructor' we simply leave the parenthesis blank, as done above.

And then, after the Employee object instance has been created, assign the object instance's reference to the object variable emp.

After this has been accomplished, any use of **emp** in the program means the Employee object instance assigned to it, or that it refers.

That is the essence in the above two code lines.

then the code line -

```
emp.Id = "Emp2002_12";
```

here we are accessing the Id property of the Employee object instance emp, by the code expression, emp.Id using the dot operator syntax and assigning it, the string value "Emp2002_12".

then the line -

```
emp.Name = "Suresh";
```

the string value "Suresh" is assigned to the object's Name property.

Based on previous explanation, it should be fairly easy to understand what is going on in the remaining lines of the code.

Note: In C#, the dot operator syntax is used to access members of a class or such similar entity definitions, that contain member definitions.

Access Modifiers:

Before we delve into other topics in this section, let us look at a critical section of programming art called Access modifiers.

*We would do well to observe in the previous code definitions the use of **public, internal** modifiers. The following paragraphs enlighten us, as to what they mean and how to use them.*

The main access modifiers in C# are:

public, internal, protected, private

Access modifiers are used to specify the accessibility scope of a member item or a code group. Elements such as class that are defined at the namespace level can be applied only public and internal access modifiers as we are not allowed to use, protected, private modifiers.

For members (methods, properties…) of elements such as class all modifiers defined are valid.

As said earlier access modifiers are used to control accessibility scope of the program items or elements such as property, field, method, class… to specific code parts of the application (assembly) they are defined in and other external application codes, based on the respective access modifiers that got applied to them.

In the following example we see method member of the Class declared as public

Code Example:

```
class Calculator
{
...
```

```
public int Result(int i, int j)
{
}
...
}
```

A member declared as **public** has the most global scope, and is accessible to any or all code in the application it is declared in, and other external application codes as well.

The second most global scope after **public** is provided by **internal**. A member declared **internal** can be accessed by all code within the assembly or namespace in which it is defined.

A **protected** member can only be accessed by all code within the class it is declared in and its sub or derived classes.

A **private** member has the least global scope in that it is accessible to code only within the class in which it is declared.

Note: When we do not explicitly declare access modifier with a member of a class, it means the member is declared private. The default access modifier is **private**.

Struct

Struct in .NET is very similar to a Class. The key difference between Struct and Class definitions is that a Class definition, results in a Reference type whereas a Struct results in a Value type.

Size consideration

We can choose a **struct** over a **class** definition when the size of the struct object is seen as fixed, and not as a varying one, and not exceeding 8 bytes. When size should exceed 8 bytes we rather go with a Class or suffer performance penalty overhead.

Notable differences between structs and classes is that a class can inherit another class but a struct cannot inherit from another struct, and, there cannot be a default constructor defined for a struct, and also, there is no Finalizer/Destructor for a struct.

Additionally, because a struct is a value type, when we assign a struct object to a struct variable of its type or pass it to a method parameter of type of the receiving struct object, a copy of the struct object is passed. So, one must be careful in its use, as in some situations it may lead to unexpected behaviour.

The syntax for working with struct is exactly the same as the syntax for working with a class, be it object instance creation, accessing members. In fact, the discussion on different member types of a class in the following topic under the sub-heading *Revisiting Classes in greater detail,* holds good with a struct definition as well.

But as noted above there cannot be a Destructor/ Finalizer for a struct. The struct object is removed or deleted, as soon as it goes out of scope.

```
Example Syntax:
struct GlobalIdee
{
//implementation code goes here
}
```

The most notable **pre-defined struct type in the .NET Framework is System.DateTime**

Enumeration

An Enumeration type defines a named group of integer constants. The following example illustrates 'enum' use.

```
Example:
enum DesignationGroup
{
Managerial, Executive, Assistant
}
```

And it is the same as

```
enum DesignationGroup
{
Managerial = 0, Executive = 1,
Assistant = 2
}
```

Revisiting Classes in greater detail

A class in essence can contain two types of sets of members, one is **data members** and the other **method**

members. Method members represent operations the class supports.

Typical data members are Fields, Events

Typical method members are Methods, Constructors, Properties, Indexers.

In the following sections we shall be looking at these to know their role and purpose. We shall also see how to define and use them.

Seeing Members as Instance and Static kind

The member types noted above can be declared as either an instance or a static member.

Instance members of a class are those that belong to, and are exclusive to an o**bject instance** and are accessible via class's object instance reference using dot operator syntax.

```
example
emp.Name
```

Static members of a class belong to Class and are accessible via Class name using dot operator syntax.

```
example
Employee.Count
```

(There is no modifier for specifying a member as **instance** member, unlike a static member for which we use the **static** modifier)

A classic example for static member is C# program's Main method, that is declared **static**. The start point of execution of an Application Program is Main() method, and, because we should access it even before we would have written a line of code to create instance of the class it is contained in, it is declared static. So that we can access it with just a reference to its' class name.

* * * * *

Fields *(data members)*

A field is a variable (also referred to as a data member) that stores a value assigned to it.

Fields are typically declared as private, using *private* access modifier.

Using *public and internal* access modifiers with fields is going against the OOP tenets of abstraction and encapsulation, that stipulate them to be private. If we do so, then we have compromised with the class's security feature.

Variants of fields; instance field, read-only field, static field, read-only static field.

A Property member acts as a security shield to a field and so, not let any code, outside the class, access it.

Properties are discussed later under Properties topic section.

Constructors

Constructor is a special method defined in a class, the sole purpose of which is to initialize the fields or data members of the class's object at the time the object is created. And the name of a constructor method should be the same as that of the class.

A constructor can be invoked only once (and not more) at the time the object is being created. Also, there is no return type associated with a constructor method because the main purpose of a constructor method is to initialize data members and not to return some object or value, as is typical with a standard **method** definition.

When we do not explicitly define a constructor for a class, then, the compiler inserts one. The compiler inserted one is called the default constructor, a zero parameter one. But the moment we explicitly define a constructor, say a parameterized one, the compiler ceases to insert the default one for us. In such a situation, we need to explicitly define the default, zero parameter one as well, if necessary.

We would do well to note that there can be overloading of the constructor method i.e. there can be more than one constructor method defined in a class, so long as we make sure that each of these constructor methods, differs in its signature with the others.

```csharp
class Employee
{
    1 reference
    public Employee() // default zero parameter Constructor
    {
        this.Id = "Not set";
        this.Name = "Not set";

    }
    0 references
    public Employee(string Id, string Name) // parameterized Constructor
    {
        this.Id = Id;
        this.Name = Name;

    }
```

Constructor code definitions

Note: If a class contains static fields that needs to be initialized through a constructor, then a static constructor would be defined for initialization of those fields by using static keyword.

Properties:

A field should be accessible only to code within class in which it is declared, and it should not be accessible to any code outside of the class. As said earlier, a **field stores data** of type specified in its declaration.

That said, typically, value for a field is assigned using a setter block, and value stored in a field is retrieved using getter block via its property member definition. The sole purpose of property definitions is to facilitate access to the fields (data members). If required, in the setter code block you can write some code to check **and validate the data value being assigned to a property.**

In other words, Properties can be seen as special method members of a class whose sole purpose is to *set values to* and *get values from* fields of the class.

Although technically, it is appropriate to see a Property member as a method type member, but without any harm we would like to see and use it as a cross, between a data type member and a method type member.

Auto-implemented Properties

Auto implemented Properties feature allows us to define properties that implicitly create data member variables corresponding to each of property members. For each auto implemented property there is a corresponding data variable (Field) inserted by the compiler, and the property facilitates *setting the value to, and getting the value from the corresponding variable.*

```
        Console.WriteLine( Emp Name:   + Name);
    }

    public string Id { get; set; }
    public string Name{ get; set; }
}
```

Code section of the above seen Employee class code showing Property definitions

Indexers

An indexer in a class is similar to a property member, but unlike a property it allows access to an array of values/ objects; as against, a single value in the case of a *Property*.

The 'this' keyword is used in defining an Indexer. So, observe the use of **'this'** in the following code example for defining an indexer.

An Indexer makes its container class behave and work like an array.

The following example declares a class that stores the designations of employees, using the DesignationGroup enum. A get accessor takes a DesignationGroup, the value of a designation group, and returns the corresponding integer. For example, DesignationGroup.Manager returns 2, DesignationGroup.Executive returns 3, and so on.

```
class DesignationInDesignationGroup
Collection
{
DesignationGroup[] desigGroups = [
DesignationGroup.Director,
DesignationGroup.AssistantDirector,
DesignationGroup.Manager,
DesignationGroup.Executive,
DesignationGroup.Assistant
];
public int this[DesignationGroup group]
=> FindDesignationGroupIndex(group);
private int FindDesignationGroupIndex
(DesignationGroup group)
{
for (int j = 0; j < desigGroups.Length;
j++)
```

```
{
if (desigGroups[j] == group)
{
return j;
}
}
throw new ArgumentOutOfRangeException(
nameof(group),
$"Designation Group {group} is not
supported.\nDesignation Group input
must be a defined DesignationGroup enum
value.");
}
}
```

Consuming preceding definition in client code:

```
var groups = new DesignationInDesignation
GroupCollection();
Console.WriteLine(groups[Designation
Group.Manager]);
try
{
Console.WriteLine(groups[(Designation
Group)22]);
}
catch (ArgumentOutOfRangeException e)
{
Console.WriteLine($"Not supported
input: {e.Message}");
}
```

*Methods:

A **method** member of a class is a block of code that stands for an operation that it implements.

To understand the value there is in a method concept, imagine this. If there didn't exist the concept of a method, we are compelled to keep writing the lines of code that stand for performing a task, repeatedly, especially when the task has to be performed multiple times in a program. This proves to be inefficient, and the program code size bloats and is also error prone and difficult to manage any changes.

Methods are the real work horses of any application.

The syntax structure of a method:

```
access-modifier return-type method-
name(parameter list of the method)
{
}
```

Method definition representation in a block diagram

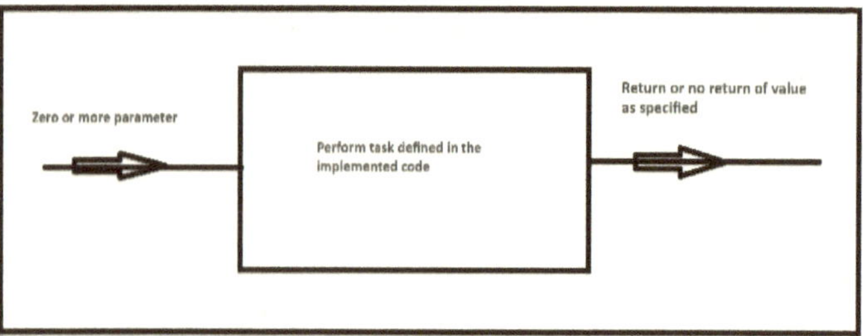

if there are no any parameter, we simply leave the parameter-list parenthesis blank or empty.

A Parameter of a method can be seen as a local variable of a method, that represents a value, that has been passed to it at the time of the method invocation. The number of parameters declared in a method can be zero, or one or more depending on the requirements of a method.

Method signature:

The parameter list i.e. the number, the order and the types of parameters, forms the signature of a method.

(There is **out**, **ref**, specifiers that can be used in a parameter declaration, there can be **varying number of parameters**, **optional parameters** but we shall not cover them here as the main focus of the book is only to address the central object-oriented programming concepts.)

Return type

If return type of a method is specified, then the method should return object or value of type specified. If a method does not return any object or value then return type should be declared as void.

Let's look at a simple and easy to understand typical Method, code definition how it looks:

Method definition code,

```
int AddNumbers(int x, int y)
{
    int result = x + y;
    return result;
}
```

As we can see this method takes two int parameter values. And the return type of the object the method should return is specified as int type. So integer object stored in the **result** variable which is sum of **x** and **y** parameter values passed to the method is returned using return statement.

Note: A variable declared inside a method is referred to as local variable and can be accessible only to code inside the method.

Check the definition of ShowPersonDetails() method – it does not declare any parameters and the return type is declared to be void, that means the method doesn't return any object.

Called/Caller sections

When we invoke any method from certain code section, the code section being executed in the called method is referred to as called section and the section from where the call was made is referred to as caller section.

When method called returns an object or value of type specified then we can accept return value, from the method call, into a variable of that object or value type being returned.

Variable declaration:

We can declare one or more variables in a method. We cannot use access modifiers for a variable declared in a method. Also, variables in a method will not be initialized by default with default values, when compared to variables/fields declared at the class level in a class. Variable declared in a method needs to be explicitly initialized by the programmer.

In the method, ShowPersonDetails(), recognize that the **prototype** of the method is:

void ShowPersonDetails();

Prototype of a method refers just to its head section, without the body.

The concept of prototype comes into play when we work with, abstract classes, interfaces and delegates.

```csharp
class Employee
{
    1 reference
    public Employee()
    {
        this.Id = "Not set";
        this.Name = "Not set";

    }
    0 references
    public Employee(string Id, string Name)
    {
        this.Id = Id;
        this.Name = Name;

    }
    1 reference
    public void ShowPersonDetails()
    {
        Console.WriteLine("Emp Id:" + Id);
        Console.WriteLine("Emp Name:" + Name);
    }

    5 references
    public string Id { get; set; }
    5 references
    public string Name{ get; set; }
}
```

Method definition code (highlighted text)

Anonymous methods

An anonymous method as the name suggests is a method definition without a name. We rely on delegate keyword to define an anonymous method.

We can also, define an anonymous method in a **Lambda Expression** format.

We may say, Lambda expression syntax has for the most part subsumed the traditional delegate anonymous method syntax.

We shall revisit these in greater detail, in the chapter Delegates and Events.

Asynchronous methods

An asynchronous method is asynchronous because, it returns immediately to the caller while it executes concurrently. We need to apply **async** modifier to a method that is asynchronous function.

Code snippet:

```
async void Test()
{
    //implementation code
}
```

await keyword:

When we call an asynchronous method, we should use await keyword with the call.

Example:

```
await Test();
```

Extension Methods

When we should see the need to define additional methods with a class, but cannot do so, as the source code of the class is not made available or inaccessible, due to the class being contained in a class library; in such a situation we could still define and associate required custom methods with the class by defining **extension methods for the class**.

Extension method definition code Example:

```
public static class RoundToTwoDecimal
{
    public static float RoundToTwoDecimal
    Places(this float x, float f)
    {

        return (float)System.Math.Round
        (f, 2);
    }
    }
```

Client class code that uses the extension method:

```
internal class Oo
{
    static void Main() {

    float f = 2.7456f;
    float f1 = f.RoundToTwoDecimalPlaces(f);
    Console.WriteLine(f1);


    }

    }
```

Observe above how a float value returned from the call to RoundToTwoDecimalPlaces method, is accepted into float type f1 variable as discussed in the called/caller section earlier.

Destructor/Finalizer

As the name suggests, Destructor method (referred to as Finalizer in .NET) is contrary in nature compared to a Constructor in that it is used for cleanup of member data objects, and results in freeing up of memory held by the member objects. Destructor/Finalizer method of an object is invoked or executed just before, when the object gets destroyed on reaching the end of its lifetime. End of lifetime of an object is when it has gone out of scope and so has lost all references to it, finished its role/job and of no use further in the remaining execution time of the program.

Garbage Collector (GC)

On reaching the end of its lifetime an object is treated as Garbage as it is not of any use. Conversely, when an object created in an executing program is finished with its purpose and of no use further, it is marked as garbage and declared to have reached the end of its lifetime and ready for disposal.

A programmer doesn't need to explicitly define a Destructor/Finalizer method, because the **Garbage Collection feature of the .NET Framework does the cleanup job automatically, without the need** for Programmer's explicit intervention by way of, writing code to perform object disposal and cleanup.

But in situations where, there is a need to explicitly handle object finalization to overcome and avoid performance penalty and program misbehaviour issues, due to a delayed GC scheme action, Programmer can explicitly implement some code to handle object disposal, using a couple of techniques provided by the Framework.

* * * * *

Static Class

A static class is a class that has only static members in it. Conversely, if a class should contain only static members in it, then we declare it as static.

Please refer to previous section *Members as Instance and Static kind* for its understanding.

A classic example of a Static class is the built-in **System.Console** class. Because there can be only one standard I/O console for a computer system, there is no point in talking about multiple Console instances for a system.

*Abstract class

An abstract class is a class that has one or more abstract method declarations in it and hence marked abstract.

The implementation job of abstract methods is of a sub-class that derives from it.

Note: When a class is a fully implemented one, it is called Concrete class and so is instantiable.

One cannot create instances of an abstract class for the simple reason, it is not fully implemented, unlike a concrete class, as it contains abstract method(s).

That said, the real value in an abstract class is that it serves as an '**abc**' meaning **a**bstract **b**ase **c**lass. And exactly that is what it is meant to be.

We shall see the significance of it later in the Inheritance chapter that follows.

Sealed Class

A class that cannot be inherited is marked sealed and so it cannot be inherited by any class.

*Interface

An interface can be seen as a class, but with one key distinction in that it consists non-implemented (abstract) method members only.

One would define an interface, heads-up when, there is knowledge of the Object types and their associated methods (operations) the interface would support, but not know how to implement them because the job of implementing the operations specified in the interface is seen by the interface as the responsibility of the classes that would see the need to do so, also in doing so, qualify to the immense benefits of dynamic interface-based polymorphism features.

A key benefit of an interface is that it serves as a contract, in the sense that, any class that implements an interface, must and should implement all the abstract methods specified in the interface. This feature allows for dynamic polymorphism. We shall study about Dynamic Polymorphism in the Polymorphism chapter that follows.

An interface can contain only abstract methods, in contrast to an abstract class which is seen as a partially implemented one, and has at least one abstract method in it.

In other words an Interface can be seen as an Abstract class with only abstract members (methods) in it.

We shall make a clear note that we cannot create instances of an Interface, but can only implement it.

In C#, there is support for only single-inheritance model, therefore, a class can inherit from only one class (called base or parent class) in a single act of inheritance, ***whereas it can implement (in some sense inherit you can say) more than one interface simultaneously.***

```
Code Example:
using System;

namespace OOPConcepts
{
    interface IPerson
{
void ShowPersonDetails();
}
    class Employee : IPerson
{
public Employee()
{
this.Id = "Not set";
this.Name = "Not set";

}
public Employee(string Id, string Name)
{
this.Id = Id;
this.Name = Name;
    }
public void ShowPersonDetails()
{
Console.WriteLine("Emp Id:" + Id);
Console.WriteLine("Emp Name:" + Name);
}
    public string Id { get; set; }
public string Name{ get; set; }
}
```

```csharp
    class Customer : IPerson
{
public Customer()
{
this.Id = "Not set";
this.Name = "Not set";
    }
public Customer(string Id, string Name)
{
this.Id = Id;
this.Name = Name;
    }
public void ShowPersonDetails()
{
Console.WriteLine("Cust Id:" + Id);
Console.WriteLine("Cust Name:" + Name);
}
    public string Id { get; set; }
public string Name { get; set; }
}
internal class Program
{
static void Main(string[] args)
{
Employee e = new Employee();
e.Id = "Emp2002_12";
e.Name = "Suresh";
if (e.Id == "Not set" && e.Name == "Not
set")
```

```csharp
Console.WriteLine("Set the values for
Id and Name properties.");
else
e.ShowPersonDetails();
Console.WriteLine();
    Customer c = new Customer();
c.Id = "Cust2002_1002";
c.Name = "Jadev";
if (c.Id == "Not set" && c.Name == "Not
set")
Console.WriteLine("Set the values Id
and Name properties.");
else
c.ShowPersonDetails();
Console.WriteLine();
    IPerson member;
//member = new Employee();
// member.ShowPersonDetails();
    member = c;
Console.WriteLine("Member selected
is:");
member.ShowPersonDetails();
    }
}
}
```

Some of the most notable interface types pre-defined in the framework are IFormattable, IEquatable, IEnumerable, IComparable, IDisposable.

Suggested Exercises

Assuming this AbcCompany is into a sales business. So, obviously Customers come into picture. Therefore think of modeling Customer, Order classes with a set of attributes that are appropriate to the sales domain. Define approriate method member definitions for the classes.

CHAPTER THREE

Delegates and Events

Delegate

Delegate is a **type safe method pointer** or reference

```
    Delegate definition code syntax:
public delegate int DelegCalculate
(int num1, int num2);
```

Having defined the delegate, we now wish to have a delegate DelegCalculate instance reference variable, point to a method (handler method) that implements target operation, and, bears a signature and a return type, that matches with the specified delegate. When observed, signature of the delegate defined above enforces that, the method takes two int parameters, and returns an int value.

Let us see the following method definition.

```
int AddNumbers(int n1, int n2)
{
return (n1 + n2);
}
```

When we examine the signature of the above method definition, we make out that, it takes two int parameters.

And return type is declared to be an int value. So, it clearly matches with the signature and the return type of the DelegCalculate delegate definition. Hence, we are able to point the DelegCalculate object reference variable to the AddNumbers method.

So, now let us write some code to do exactly that.

```
DelegCalculate calc = new DelegCalculate
(AddNumbers);
```

Having done so, we can now invoke the AddNumbers method through the delegate object reference as in the following code.

```
int sum = calc(20,40);
Console.WriteLine(sum); // prints 60
```

Using an Anonymous method:

An anonymous method is one that is not named.

In cases where handler method exists just as an executing expression that is executed when the delegate is invoked, we can go for an **anonymous method**. A method without name is directly attached to a delegate variable.

Using this, our above code will change to:

```
DelegCalculate calc;
calc = delegate (int n1, int n2)
{return (n1 + n2);};
Invoke code:
calc(20,40);
```

A **lambda expression** as said earlier in the previous chapter, is another form of expressing an anonymous method.

Using Lambda Expression,

If we were to implement the above in Lambda expression format then it would be:

```
calc = (n1, n2) => n1 + n2;
Invoke code:
calc(20, 40);
Lambda syntax:
```

Events and Event Handling

An event is any action that triggers an event of interest.

It should be quite interesting to note that all Event handling in .NET is based on the concept of Delegates. Without Delegates no event handling is possible.

Event handling is the act of having a method - whose signature and return type matches with event delegate - wired or bound to an event member of a specified delegate type; this method, bound to an event is then referred to as **event method,** and will be invoked on trigger of that event.

The discussion in the above paragraph clearly reveals that events and event-handling is based on a Publisher/ Subscriber model.

In real world, we recognize most applications use or depend on a Publisher/Subscriber model.

Typical example of the Publisher/Subscriber model would be the ubiquitous Button click event and the handling of that (in doing something in response to click of the Button).

It may be explained as:

The Button object publishes an event member named **click** and there exists a client method that subscribes to the click event, when the click event occurs, the client event method is called and executed. Thus, the event method performs the operation defined in it, in response to the fired click event.

So, referring to our Delegate example seen and discussed earlier in the beginning of this chapter, if we are, now to declare an event member with the name **addNums,** of the above DelegCalculate type, it would be as follows:

```
public event DelegCalculate addNums;
```

Then the code to bind AddNumbers event handler method to this event, would be:

```
addNums += AddNumbers
```

Refer to Generic EventHandler Delegate event example code appended at the end of Appendix B.

Suggested Exercise

Refer to sample Generic EventHandler delegate for an event member of the HR application code appended at the end of the book for a practical for understanding typically, how events and event handling is performed in a .NET Application.

CHAPTER FOUR

Inheritance

Inheritance is one of the key characteristics or features of Object-Oriented Programming.

As said earlier, "***Inheritance*** is the ability to extend the features of an existing pre-defined Class, in a new Class being defined". That is, the new class being defined inherits an existing pre-defined class.

"The most useful result of inheritance is code reusability besides providing the ability to structure related classes in a hierarchy, called object model."

Where we can see a 'is a' relationship exist between two objects, there we can employ inheritance.

*Every Fulltime-Employee **is a** Employee*

Because we see that a 'is a' relationship holds between FulltimeEmployee and Employee objects, we can apply inheritance between these objects.

In standard jargon, terms used to refer to a base class are ***base*** or ***parent*** or ***super*** class. For the derived class i.e. the class that inherits a base class are referred as ***derived*** or ***child*** or ***sub*** class. But they all mean one and the same.

The implementation of inheritance in C# is:

General Syntax:

```
class NewDerivedClass :
ExistingBaseClass {}
Code Example:
class Employee
{
//employee code definitions here...
}
class FulltimeEmployee : Employee
{
// code here
}
```

In the previous code block we see that this new FulltimeEmployee class inherits from the base Employee class. The colon ':' is the inheritance operator by which inheritance is implemented.

Another example

```
class ParttimeEmployee : Employee
{
//implementation code here
}
```

Declaring a method as virtual in base class allows it to be overridden in a derived class.

```csharp
    class Employee
{
public Employee()
{
this.Id = "Not set";
this.Name = "Not set";
}
    public Employee(string Id, string Name)
{
this.Id = Id;
this.Name = Name;
}
    public void ShowPersonDetails()
{
Console.WriteLine("Emp Id:" + Id);
Console.WriteLine("Emp Name:" + Name);
}
    public virtual decimal CalculatePay()
    {
    return (Basic + OtherAllowance);
    }
    public string Id { get; set; }
public string Name{ get; set; }


}


    class FullTimeEmployee : Employee
{
public FullTimeEmployee()
```

```csharp
{
this.Basic= 0.00M;
this.HouseRentAllowance = 0.00M;
this.OtherAllowance = 0.00M;
}
public FullTimeEmployee(decimal basic,
decimal hra, decimal otherAllowance)
{
this.Basic= basic;
this.HouseRentAllowance = hra;
this.OtherAllowance = otherAllowance;
}
   public override decimal CalculatePay()
{
return (Basic + HouseRentAllowance +
OtherAllowance);
}

public decimal Basic{ get; set; }
public decimal HouseRentAllowance{ get;
set; }
public decimal OtherAllowance{ get;
set; }
}
```

   The client code for the class:

```csharp
internal class Program
{
```

```csharp
static void Main()
{
FullTimeEmployee fullTimeEmployee = new
FullTimeEmployee();
fullTimeEmployee.Id = "2004";
fullTimeEmployee.Name = "Bhaj";
fullTimeEmployee.Basic = 12000.00M;
fullTimeEmployee.HouseRentAllowance =
5000.00M;
fullTimeEmployee.OtherAllowance =
5000.00M;
decimal payAmt = fullTimeEmployee.
CalculatePay();
Console.WriteLine($"Pay Amount {payAmt} ");
}
    }
```

Abstract class and Inheritance

For a class to qualify as an abstract class there has to be at least one abstract method specified in it. To understand this principle in play, we shall modify and redefine the Employee class defined previously, to contain an abstract method and be qualified as an Abstract class. We use abstract keyword for this purpose.

Because an abstract class contains one or more abstract methods, we cannot create instances of it, but it serves as a base class.

```csharp
   abstract class Employee
{
public Employee()
{
this.Id = "Not set";
this.Name = "Not set";
}
   public Employee(string Id, string Name)
{
this.Id = Id;
this.Name = Name;
}
   public void ShowPersonDetails()
{
Console.WriteLine("Emp Id:" + Id);
Console.WriteLine("Emp Name:" + Name);
}
   public abstract decimal CalculatePay();
   public string Id { get; set; }
public string Name{ get; set; }


}
   class FullTimeEmployee : Employee
{
public FullTimeEmployee()
{
this.Basic= 0.00M;
this.HouseRentAllowance = 0.00M;
this.OtherAllowance = 0.00M;
}
```

```csharp
public FullTimeEmployee(decimal basic,
decimal hra, decimal otherAllowance)
{
this.Basic= basic;
this.HouseRentAllowance = hra;
this.OtherAllowance = otherAllowance;
}
    public override decimal CalculatePay()
{
return (Basic + HouseRentAllowance +
OtherAllowance);
}

public decimal Basic{ get; set; }
public decimal HouseRentAllowance{ get;
set; }
public decimal OtherAllowance{ get;
set; }
}
```

The client code for the class:

```csharp
internal class Program
{
static void Main()
{
FullTimeEmployee fullTimeEmployee = new
FullTimeEmployee();
fullTimeEmployee.Id = "2004";
fullTimeEmployee.Name = "Bhaj";
```

```
fullTimeEmployee.Basic = 12000.00M;
fullTimeEmployee.HouseRentAllowance =
5000.00M;
fullTimeEmployee.OtherAllowance =
5000.00M;
decimal payAmt = fullTimeEmployee.
CalculatePay();
Console.WriteLine($"Pay Amount {payAmt}
");
}
    }
```

the output:

Program output

Observe the use of abstract specifier with the CalculatePay method.

Now because the Employee class contains this abstract method. The class should be explicitly declared abstract as well. It is a must.

Then we have FullTimeEmployee class (concrete class) override, the CalculatePay() abstract method of its base class Employee, to have its own implementation of the method.

So, an abstract method in a base class is for a derived class to override and implement.

Also observe in the Client class code, we are able to access the Id and Name properties of the base class using the derived class object reference in the code lines,

```
fullTimeEmployee.Id = "2004";
fullTimeEmployee.Name = "Bhaj";
```

This clearly illustrates that **members of the base class are all inherited by the derived class** (including private members, though not accessible) **by virtue of Inheritance.**

So, a derived class is all that its base class is and something more.

Derived class is to be seen as a specialization of its base class, that can include its own member definitions apart from those derived from the base class.

In the derived class code, if we should access any base class member, we can do so using the **'base'** keyword

Do It Yourself exercise:

(This other ParttimeEmployee class we saw earlier can also be derived from Employee abstract base class, and then go on to have its own implementation of CalculatePay() method, and perform a calculation like NoOfHoursWorked x HourlyRate).

Order of Constructor methods invocation (of base class, sub class..)

When we create an object instance of a sub class type, we should understand that, first base class object members would be created and initialized through the base class constructor and then the sub class members, so therefore, first base class constructor would be invoked/executed then the sub class one. Bit of logical sense can help us understand that it should be rightfully so.

Constructor chaining

Constructor chaining is the ability to specify/create an invocation chain of constructors, from one constructor to another. It could even involve chaining a specific base class constructor from a sub class constructor.

Casting

Casting is converting an object of a type to its Compatible type.

There are two ways of casting and those are Up Casting and DownCasting

Upcasting takes place implicitly. In the example above we assigned FulltimeEmployee object to its base type i.e Employee type variable; this is upcasting.

Down casting is to be performed explicitly i.e. when Employee type object variable stores FulltimeEmployee object instance and we need to assign it to an object variable of type FulltimeEmployee.

Code Example

```
Employee emp1 = new FulltimeEmployee();
FulltimeEmployee fulltimeEmp1 =
(FulltimeEmployee)emp1;
```

Observe the casting in the right-hand side expression where we cast emp1 variable to FulltimeEmployee type. This is performed when a base type variable holds sub-type object and so is being cast to the appropriate sub-type variable when being assigned.

Suggested Exercises

Try extending knowledge gained in Suggested Excercises of the previous chapter. Think of the possibilities of extending Customer and Order (Sale Order) - applying inheritance principles learnt in the chapter. Ponder over the candidate methods of the derived classes for Customer and Order objects.

CHAPTER FIVE

Polymorphism

Polymorphism is the ability to have a single operation support multiple implementations.

There are basically two forms of Polymorphism static and dynamic.

Method overloading is a form of static polymorphism.

Refer to Employee Code Example in the first chapter. Constructor methods have been overloaded. Based on the parameters passed in a constructor call, the constructor method that would be invoked is resolved, and this knowledge is available at the compile time itself, so it is a static form of polymorphism.

Method overriding and interface-based polymorphism are forms of dynamic polymorphism

Refer to code example of the Employee class definition with virtual method section in the previous Inheritance chapter, for the illustration of Method overriding. Now the key point is that, because FulltimeEmployee class is derived from Employee class, and based on the 'is a' relationship logic discussed in the Inheritance chapter, it is perfectly valid to declare an object variable of type Employee and then go on to assign to it, a reference of its sub-type object, that is FulltimeEmployee object instance. Let us implement that in the code as follows.

```
Employee emp = new FulltimeEmployee();
    emp.Id = "2004";
    emp.Name = "Bhaj";
    emp.Basic = 12000.00M;
    emp.HouseRentAllowance = 5000.00M;
    emp.OtherAllowance = 5000.00M;
```

Having done so, let us try to invoke CalculatePay() method and observe the result. Let us do so, by writing the code as follows:

```
emp.CalculatePay();
```

On running the program we see the following output:

Program output

So, what we are seeing in the output is the result of invoking the CalculatePay() method of the FulltimeEmployee class and not that of Employee class, although emp variable, has been declared to be of type Employee class. So, it is not the type of the object variable that will determine which CalculatePay method would be invoked (whether of base class or derived class). It is the object that it points to, that will determine it. Now because, the object pointed to in this case is that of FulltimeEmployee, it will invoke CalculatePay method of FulltimeEmployee class. And this is resolved dynamically at the runtime, therefore this is dynamic form of polymorphism.

Make a note also, that **declaring a method as abstract in a base class is similar to a virtual method** and is done with a view to seeing it overridden in a derived class. **But the difference between declaring a method member as virtual and abstract is that, virtual method would have implementation whereas abstract method is without any implementation and so abstract.** Otherwise, both are very similar in their workings with regard to dynamic polymorphism discussed in the preceding paragraph.

Declaring an object variable of an interface type, is akin to declaring a variable of an abstract class type. And it offers dynamic polymorphism features applied/ discussed in the preceding paragraphs.

code example of interface based dynamic polymorphism.

using System;

```
namespace OOPConcepts
{
    interface IPerson
{
void ShowPersonDetails();
}
```

```csharp
    class Employee : IPerson
{
public Employee()
{
this.Id = "Not set";
this.Name = "Not set";


}
public Employee(string Id, string Name)
{
this.Id = Id;
this.Name = Name;
    }
public void ShowPersonDetails()
{
Console.WriteLine("Emp Id:" + Id);
Console.WriteLine("Emp Name:" + Name);
}
    public string Id { get; set; }
public string Name{ get; set; }
}
    class Customer : IPerson
{
public Customer()
{
this.Id = "Not set";
this.Name = "Not set";
    }
public Customer(string Id, string Name)
```

```
{
this.Id = Id;
this.Name = Name;
    }
public void ShowPersonDetails()
{
Console.WriteLine("Cust Id:" + Id);
Console.WriteLine("Cust Name:" + Name);
}
    public string Id { get; set; }
public string Name { get; set; }
    }
internal class Program
{
static void Main(string[] args)
{
Employee e = new Employee();
e.Id = "Emp2002_12";
e.Name = "Suresh";
if (e.Id == "Not set" && e.Name == "Not
set")
Console.WriteLine("Please, set the values
first for Emp Id and Name properties.");
else
e.ShowPersonDetails();
Console.WriteLine();
    Customer c = new Customer();
c.Id = "Cust2002_1002";
c.Name = "Jadev";
```

```csharp
if (c.Id == "Not set" && c.Name == "Not
set")
Console.WriteLine("Please, set the values
first for Emp Id and Name properties.");
else
c.ShowPersonDetails();
Console.WriteLine();
    IPerson member;
member = new Employee();
member.ShowPersonDetails();
    member = c;
Console.WriteLine("Member selected
is:");
member.ShowPersonDetails();
    }
}
}
```

Suggested Exercises

Think of defining interfaces and abstract classes and the possible abstract method candidates for the Customer and Order objects. Apply thought to the possibilities of dynamic polymorphism going through a few examples through a research conducted for the purpose.

Explore on Operator Overloading. And is it static form or dynamic form of polymorphism?

Explore on what Method Hiding means in a Inheritance based derived class.

CHAPTER SIX

Generics

Generics implement and strengthen the polymorphism feature of OOP.

A **Generic** is a **Parameterized Type** that allows its members operate on any other type of object.

C# (.NET) generics feature enables us associate polymorphic behaviour with a Class.

The example that follows, illustrates the prime value in a Generic type.

First let's look at, a Non-generic version of a class, and then after that go on to implement a Generic version of it, so that we can truly appreciate the real value there is, in a Generic class.

```
Non-generic:
class NonGenericVersion
{
object _t1 ;
object _t2;
public NonGenericVersion(object t1,
object t2)
{
_t1 = t1;
```

```
_t2 = t2;
}
}
Generic version:
class GenericVersion<T1, T2>
{
T1 _t1;
T2 _t2;
public GenericVersion(T1 t1, T2 t2)
{
_t1 = t1;
_t2 = t2;
}
}
Declare and define a Generic method;
static void Swap<T>(ref T lhs, ref T rhs)
{
T temp;
temp = lhs;
lhs = rhs;
rhs = temp;
}
```

Having defined the Generic method we now use it in the following code example ;

We will use TestSwap() method to swap two int values;

```
public static void TestSwap()
{
int a = 1;
```

```
int b = 2;
Swap<int>(ref a, ref b);
System.Console.WriteLine(a + " " + b);
}
```

We will modify TestSwap() method to work with float values;

```
public static void TestSwap()
{
float a = 1.23;
float b = 2.24;
Swap<float>(ref a, ref b);
System.Console.WriteLine(a + " " + b);
}
```

Clear Note:- As the preceding example illustrates, when the functionality offered by a class should remain the same, irrespective of the type of data objects it operates on, then Generics help us accomplish it effortlessly.

CHAPTER SEVEN

Collections

Both Non-generic collections and Generic collections are discussed in this topic.

After working with Generic collections provided by the .NET Framework one would rightly realize that Generic collections flourish, simply for the practical value they provide in real time applications development.

Generic collections are more efficient both in terms of programmer effort and execution performance than their Non-Generic counterparts.

So that said, What is a collection?

A collection means a group or set of items.

For example, we say I have a collection of coins. I have a great collection of stamps. I have collection of hit song albums. I have a nice collection of pictures.

These all refer to a set or group of items. A collection means a group of items.

Non-Generic Collections:

The System.Collections namespace provides a set of Non-generic Collection classes, notable among these is an ArrayList class, using which we can dynamically build a list of objects.

Using ArrayList

Code Example:

```
ArrayList al = new ArrayList();
al.Add("Hello");
al.Add("World");
al.Add(5);
Console.WriteLine("The array has " +
al.Count + " items");
foreach(object ob in al)
Console.WriteLine(ob.ToString());
```

As we can see in the preceding code, we could add any type of object to ArrayList. It is taken as generic Object type. So, this proves the point that Non-generic collections are not type-safe whereas Generic collections provide type safety. And also, when an item in ArrayList has to be processed, the programmer has to take care of type-casting it to the **type of object, the item is**.

So, type safety feature is where Generic Collections score over Non-generic Collections.

Generic Collections:

Some of the most notable built-in Generic Collection classes are

List<T>, Dictionary<Tkey, Tvalue>, Queue<T>, Stack<T>, Set

Let's go on to understand each of these in the same order we mentioned, as we explore and understand them.

Illustration examples for List<T>:

To work with a list of integer objects with the List<T>, we simply specify int type as a parameter to the List<T> class. Then having done so we can add integer objects to the list by invoking Add() method of the list object.

```
List<int> integers = new List<int>();
integers.Add(0);
integers.Add(10);
integers.Add(20);
```

Having added integers to the list object, we can access each of them using *foreach* statement as follows:

```
foreach(int i in integers)
Console.WriteLine(i);
```

Similarly,

To work with a list of string objects with List<T> class, we simply specify string type as a parameter to the list class. Doing so, we can add string objects to the list by invoking Add() method of the list object.

```
List<string> strings = new
List<string>();
strings.Add("Yesterday");
```

```
strings.Add("Today");
strings.Add("Tomorrow");
foreach (string strValue in strings)
Console.WriteLine(strValue);
```

Similarly, for working with Employee objects:

```
    List<Employee> employees =
    new List<Employee>();
employees.Add(new Employee("Emp20120012",
"Dikku"));
employees.Add(new Employee("Emp20240042",
"Bikhu"));
    foreach (Employee employee in
    employees) {
Console.WriteLine($"Employee Name
{employee.Name}");
Console.WriteLine($"Employee Id
{employee.Id}");
```

As seen above, the real value in a List<T> object is that it can dynamically grow in size as we keep adding the objects, and the beauty is, we are working with the same List<T> class for different object lists.

So, this is the **polymorphic behaviour in a Generic List (as appreciated in the preceding Generics chapter).** The type of objects that would be stored in the list is being specified as a parameter to the List<T> class. So, we should understand that T is just a place holder for the type of object involved. If we should work with int objects, we simply specify **int** as parameter, which would replace T with int.

Similarly, when we should work with string objects, we simply specify **string** as parameter, which would replace T with string.

We use Add() method to add items to list, Remove() method to remove items from the list.

If we should remove a string object from above created strings list, we invoke the Remove method,

```
strings.Remove("Yesterday");
```

So in this case, the first occurrence of the string object with the value "Yesterday" would be deleted or removed from the list.

Dictionary<Tkey, Tvalue>

A dictionay object stores key-value pairs.

To understand what this means let's consider a common thing, a Dictionary book. Dictionary stores a list of words with their meanings (it is a big list of *word and word meaning* pairs). So, we can see a word as a key and its meaning as a value. It is akin to key-value pairs of a collection dictionary object mentioned above.

We work with such Dictionary objects in C# using the collection object

Dictionary<Tkey, Tvalue>

Code Example:

```
   var classDetails = new System.
   Collections.Generic.Dictionary<string,
   string>();
classDetails.Add("Person class",
"Represents Person attributes and
methods");
classDetails.Add("Employee class",
"Represents Employee attributes and
methods");
classDetails.Add("Customer class",
"Represents Customer attributes and
methods");
   foreach(KeyValuePair<string, string>
   kvp in classDetails)
{ Console.WriteLine(kvp.Key + "- " +
kvp.Value);}
```

Queue<T>

When we should work with a list of objects in a queue behaviour, we can use Queue<T>. A queue object is a first-in-first-out (FIFO) structure. So let us see, how to work with Queue<T> class.

```
   var queue = new Queue<Employee>();
queue.Enqueue(new Employee("Emp200814",
"Puri"));
```

```
queue.Enqueue(new Employee("Emp200815",
"Paary"));
queue.Enqueue(new Employee("Emp200816",
"Gary"));
    foreach (Employee item in queue)
Console.WriteLine(item.Id + " " + item.
Name);
    queue.Dequeue();
    foreach (Employee item in queue)
Console.WriteLine(item.Id + " " + item.
Name);
```

Stack<T>

If a Queue is about First-In-First-Out, then Stack implements Last-In-First-Out (LIFO) structure;

```
//stack
var stack = new Stack<Employee>();
stack.Push(new Employee("Emp200814",
"Puri"));
stack.Push(new Employee("Emp200815",
"Paary"));
stack.Push(new Employee("Emp200816",
"Gary"));
    Console.WriteLine("Stack example");
    foreach (Employee item in stack)
Console.WriteLine(item.Id + " " + item.
Name);
    stack.Pop();
    foreach (Employee item in stack)
```

```
Console.WriteLine(item.Id + " " + item.
Name);
```

Sets

We would work with *Sets* when set operations such as union, intersection is to be performed between two collections.

Note:-Although arrays can be used for this sort of purpose, arrays cannot dynamically grow like this Lists do. When we declare and create an array, we should be specifying the size (number of elements or objects array stores) of the array explicitly (or implicitly through assignment of values/objects).

So, we can say, *Array object* is no good, when we should work with dynamic lists that can grow and shrink at the runtime. Arrays are discussed in the following chapter.

CHAPTER EIGHT

Arrays and Strings

Arrays

An **array** is similar to **collection** objects that we have studied in the previous chapter, as it represents a collection of values/objects. But the fundamental difference between collections and arrays is that, size of an array (number of elements/objects it stores) should be declared at the time the array object is created. So, we can say, size of an **array** is known at the compile time itself and remains fixed, in contrast to **collections** whose size can be varied dynamically at the runtime. So, unless we know pretty well that the number of elements/objects an array would store, is fixed and does not vary, we wouldn't prefer an array. Otherwise, we go with a collection which offers the flexibility of dynamically varying its size at the runtime.

Code Example:

```
int[] nums = new int[4];
nums[0] = 1;
nums[1] = 2;
nums[2] = 3;
nums[3] = 4;
```

Notice the use of index for accessing each of the elements in the array. Arrays are indexed objects.

The index used for accessing the first element is 0. The index used for accessing the second element is 1 and so on..

The index of the last element is one less than the size of the array.

In general, we can say the range of indices is, 0 to n-1, where n is the number of elements in an array.

If we should implicitly determine the size by way of initializing the array with values, we can do it as follows,

```
int[] nums = {1, 2, 3, 4};
```

The size of the **nums** array is 4, because 4 integer objects are assigned to it. This is, implicitly determining the size of an array.

Array objects support a very useful property, *Length.*

So to know the number of elements in nums, we can do so with the following:

```
Console.WriteLine($"no. of integers = {nums.Length}");
```

Similarly if we should work with an array of strings,

```
string[] strings = new string[3]
{"Hello","world", "beautiful"};
```

```
foreach (string str in strings)
Console.WriteLine(str);
```

Multi-Dimensional Arrays

What we saw till this point were single-dimensional arrays. We can have, more than one-dimension ones, which are referred to as multi-dimensional arrays.

example:

```
int[,] intNumbers = new int[2, 4] { {
1, 2, 3, 4 },{5, 6, 7, 8 } };
   for (int i = 0; i < 2; i++)
{
   for (int j = 0; j < 4; j++)
{
   Console.WriteLine("Value[{0} , {1}]
   = {2}" , i, j, intNumbers[i,j]);
   }
   }
```

```
Value[0 , 0]  = 1
Value[0 , 1]  = 2
Value[0 , 2]  = 3
Value[0 , 3]  = 4
Value[1 , 0]  = 5
Value[1 , 1]  = 6
Value[1 , 2]  = 7
Value[1 , 3]  = 8
```

multi-dimensional arrays

Jagged Arrays:

We would wrap and leave the arrays section just with a note that Jagged Arrays can be seen as an array of arrays.

Strings

A string is a sequence of zero or more characters enclosed in double quotes.

"Hello!" is a string value.

code example

```
string greetings = "Hello World";
```

Notice that although a string is a reference type, we work with it as if it is a simple value type (that is to say **we do not use** *new* **operator keyword** for creating a new string instance).

We can also see a string as an array of characters:

```
Console.WriteLine($"The first character
in greetings string variable is
{greetings[0]}");
Console.WriteLine($"The seventh character
in greetings string variable is
{greetings[6]}");
```

Process a string using *for*, *foreach* statements as follows:

```
for(int i = 0; i < greetings.Length; i++)
Console.WriteLine(greetings[i]);
foreach(char ch in greetings)
Console.WriteLine(ch);
```

We can **concatenate** two strings using the '**+**' operator;

```
string s = "One " + "Four";
string s1 = "One";
string s2 = "Two";
s = s1 + s2;
```

Strings are immutable

In the previous code line, we are changing the string value stored in the variable s, by assigning it a new value. But the point is, contrary to what one would expect, there is **no any overwrite, and replacement** of the string value held in s, with the assigned new value. In reality, what happens is that a new string object with the assigned value would be created and then its reference assigned to s. And the previous string value held in s, would be regarded garbage, and so ready for disposal, (assuming there are no any other references to it).

What was explained above, points to the **immutable** nature of a string value. **Strings are immutable**. What this means is that **once a string object has been created there is no way we can modify/change it.**

We would do well to say this again that, **assignment of a different string value** to change the value held **in a string variable, results in the creation of a new string object with the assigned value, and then, the reference (or address) of this new string object, is assigned to the string variable.**

Some useful methods supported by string object

Yet another way to **concatenate** strings is by using the **Conca**t method of the String class.

```
string ResultStr = string.Concat(s1, s2);
```

If we want to make a copy of a string we can do it as in the example below:

```
string stringCopy = string.Copy(s3);
```

Compare two string values

We can use the Compare() method of string class to compare two strings. This method returns an integer value, this integer value returned will be one of these, **positive or negative or a zero.**

So, positive integer value means the first string's value is greater (in alphabetic order) than the second one.

Negative integer value means the first string's value is less (in alphabetic order) than the second one.

Zero means both the string values are equal.

```
int res = string.Compare("Two", "One");
Console.WriteLine(res);
res = string.Compare("Two", "Two");
Console.WriteLine(res);
```

Padding

If we would want to add spaces to a string at the beginning, we can do so using PadLeft method

Code:

```
string s = "Hello"
strResult = s.PadLeft(10);
```

10 indicates the length of the string.

The above line would cause the string value in s to be right-aligned and then (10 - length of s) number of character spaces, filled with whitespaces on leftside.

If we should append '*' characters to a string at the end, we would use PadRight method.

Code:

```
strResult = s.PadRight(12, '*');
```

Trimming

In some requirements, we would want to remove whitespaces, then in that case Trim() can be used.

To remove whitespaces at the beggining, TrimStart()

To remove whitespaces at the end, TrimEnd()

Code:

```
   string strResult;
string sHello = " Hello-- ";
Console.WriteLine($"{sHello}");
   strResult = sHello.TrimStart();
   Console.WriteLine($"{strResult}");
```

Extracting strings from a given string using IndexOf(), LastIndexOf()

```
string sHello = " Hello-- ";


int bgnCharIndex = sHello.IndexOf('H');
int endCharIndex = sHello.
LastIndexOf('o');
string newSubstringExtract = sHello.
Substring(bgnCharIndex, endCharIndex);


    Console.WriteLine(newSubstring
    Extract);
  //Console.WriteLine($"{sHello.IndexOf
  ("e")}");
//Console.WriteLine($"{sHello.LastIndexOf
("l")}");
```

Probing a string for specific values using Contains(), StartsWith() EndsWith() methods

```
   Console.WriteLine(sHello.Contains
   ("ello"));
Console.WriteLine(sHello.StartsWith(" "));
```

Modifying Strings

Insert a string or character into an existing string using Insert() method

```
    strResult = sHello.Insert(6, "o");
Console.WriteLine($"{strResult}");
```

Split, Join strings

Split() method use

```
    string[] strItems = sHello.Split(" ");
foreach (string item in strItems)
Console.WriteLine(item);
```

Join() method use

```
    strResult = string.Join(" ", strItems);
Console.WriteLine(strResult.ToString());
```

StringBuilder

StringBuilder class is contained in the System.Text namespace. When we should manipulate a string say, repeatedly in an additive assignment (concatenate strings repeatedly), then we rather go with StringBuilder class, as it is more efficient, as it doesn't involve the overhead of creating new string object in each of the additive assignment operations.

Regular Expressions

Regular expressions feature helps us inspect and look for a match for a pattern in a string value. The namespace that contains the **RegEx** class is **System. Text.RegularExpressions.**

Example:

email id - string value has a certain standard pattern, so we can check for the pattern using regular expression. Example code follows:

Codeline to invoke below method would be -

```
bool validEmailId = ValidateEmail
 ("chenna@americaonline.com");
```

```
string emailPattern = @"^[a-zA-Z0-9._%+-]
+@[a-zA-Z0-9.-]+\.[a-zA-Z]{2,}$";
public bool ValidateEmail(string email)
{
if (email.IsNullOrEmpty())
return false;
Regex regex = new Regex(emailPattern);
bool m = regex.IsMatch(email);
return m;
}
```

phone - phone number is another string value in which we can check for the existence of a pattern using a regular expression. phone number (###) ###-#### format.

Example:

```
Regex regex = new Regex(@"^\(?(\d{3})\)?
[\s\-]?(\d{3})\-?(\d{4})$");
bool m = regex.IsMatch("(642)-346-7489");
Console.WriteLine(m);
```

CHAPTER NINE

Exceptions and Exception Handling

An **exception** is a runtime error.

While writing a program, we should be mindful of three types of errors that are possible, and they are **design time errors, compile time errors** and **runtime errors**. When we work with code editors such as visual studio, the intelligent editing environment provides an IntelliSense feature that will prompt errors and error correction suggestions while writing the code itself. **So, these are design time errors**. Compile time errors are those that result when we compile the code. **These are compile-time errors. We should fix these errors before we can successfully compile the code without any errors and be able to run the program. While runtime errors are those that we encounter when the program is running or in execution.**

The act of handling an exception, referred to as **exception handling** is implemented by, a set of standard code block structures, using a set of keywords defined for this purpose.

Exception Handling Mechanism allows smooth and safe exit from the program, if in a application error condition, and at the same time let the user know the condition through a clear and friendly message rather than leave the user annoyed and confused over abrupt end of the program due to the error.

The keywords are *try, catch, finally, throw*

Every exception class is derived from the base System. Exception class

Notable built-in exception classes provided by the framework are DivideByZeroException, NullReferenceException, IndexOutOfRangeException, FileNotFoundException..

all derived from base Exception class

code example

```
    internal class Program
{
static void Main()
{
int[] BookLeaves = new int[4] { 1, 2,
3, 4 };
try
{
for (int i = 0; i < 7; i++)
{
```

```
    Console.WriteLine($"Book leaf no.
    {BookLeaves[i]}");
}


}
catch (Exception e) {
Console.WriteLine("{0}" , e.Message);


}
    finally
    {
    Console.WriteLine("Perform resource
    cleanup code here");
    }
    ****||****
```

There can be more than one **catch** block corresponding to a single **try** block. Following is the example that illustrates that. When writing more than one catch block, the most specific ones (in this case IndexOutOfRange) should be placed above, then the most generic one (that is Exception class) should come at the bottom below. In the below code block you can notice that we anticipate a IndexOutOfRange which is plausible given its context, so we have written catch block corresponding to IndexOutOfRange. Also, we shall make a note that, it is quite possible that a single try block code produce more than one type of error. So, when we can anticipate the specific types of errors that could result, we shall write their corresponding **catch code blocks** and **these shall be placed above, the generic *Exception class* catch code block, because the generic Exception code block can catch any type of error, as all Exception classes are derived from the base, generic Exception class.**

Note: Even *try-catch blocks* can be nested.

Code:

```
    internal class Program
{
static void Main()
{
int[] BookLeaves = new int[4] { 1, 2,
3, 4 };
try
{
for (int i = 0; i < 7; i++)
{
   Console.WriteLine($"Book leaf no.
   {BookLeaves[i]}");
}


}
    catch (IndexOutOfRangeException e) {
Console.WriteLine("{0}" , e.Message);

}
```

```
catch (Exception e) {
Console.WriteLine("{0}" , e.Message);


}
   finally
   {
   Console.WriteLine("Perform resource
   cleanup code here");
   }
   ****||****
```

For *throw* usage check the code in the indexer topic, to understand the use of *throw* statement.

Custom Exceptions

If you see the need for application based, application specific custom exception handling then you can define an exception class for that purpose. But make sure that it is derived from the built-in base ApplicationException class

code syntax:

```
class ValueException : ApplicatioException
{
//Implementation code here
}
```

CHAPTER TEN

Reflection

Reflection feature allows a programmer discover or obtain, a type's information dynamically at the runtime.

Every object type supports the GetType() method that is inherited from the Object type. Read through the Appendix A section to get the idea of what this means.

Also, there is a built-in **System.Type** type provided by the Framework that we can use to obtain the information of a type. **The GetType() method of an object returns this System.Type object**.

Actually, there is more than one way to get to Type type object; other common way is to use *typeof()* operator. We would see it in play in the **attributes based coding** section that follows.

So, what we do now is, declare a variable by name 'type' and it is of type, **'Type'**. Then we will have this variable store the **Type** type object returned by invoking the mpObj object's GetType() method. Now using this **Type** type object we can obtain information, of the object members and their specification details.

```csharp
1   using System;
2   using System.Collections.Generic;
3   using System.Linq;
4   using System.Text;
5   using System.Threading.Tasks;
6   using InterfacesAndClasses;
7   using System.Runtime;
8   using System.Reflection;
9
10  namespace ReflectionCode
11  {
12
13      class MyPObj
14      { private int ID; private string? Name; private string? Description; }
15      internal class ReflectionCodeExampleProgram
16      {
17          static void Main()
18          {
19              MyPObj mpObj = new MyPObj();
20
21              Type type = mpObj.GetType();
22
23              Console.WriteLine(type.FullName);
24              foreach (FieldInfo field in type.GetFields(BindingFlags.NonPublic | BindingFlags.Instance))
25              { Console.WriteLine(field.Name); }
26          }
27
28      }
29  }
30
```

Reflection of MyPObj

Output:

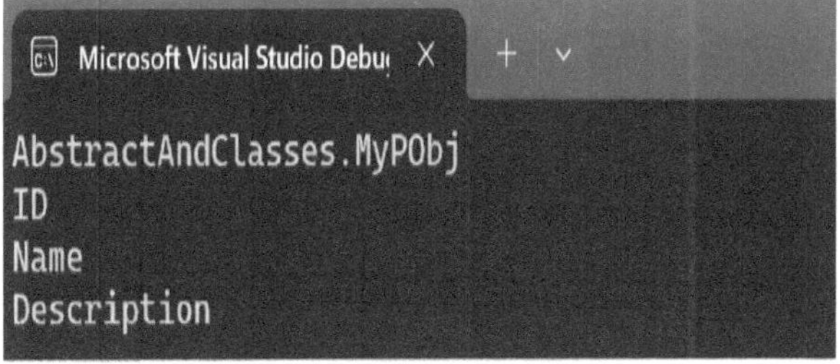

Above reflection program output

As we can see Type object supports method GetFields() to obtain fields info of the MyPobj.

Similarly, it supports GetMethods(), GetProperties().... We can invoke these methods to obtain information about the methods and properties defined in the object, and such.

This feature is appropriately named as Reflection because this **Type** type object acts like a mirror and it reflects the type information of the object presented to it.

Attributes based coding

Attributes based programming allows attach attribute tags defined, to program elements/ blocks such as class, method, property, constructor. This feature simplifies writing program code. It is kind of write less and do more and can be seen as an elegant way of writing code.

The following code example shows how we can intercept attribute tags attached to the class CustomerEmployee and its' method member AssignPrivilege(). This is just a demonstration of how attributes-based programming can be used.

Also, note that we have not implemented any code in the AssignPrivilege() method for taking appropriate 'Assign Privilege' action when the method is invoked by a employee a user who is found to be a senior and so has the authorization to perform assigning of privileges. The code for AssignPrivilege() method can be implemented according to the requirements of the application.

Defining an attribute

```
public enum Skill { Senior, Junior}
[AttributeUsage( AttributeTargets.All)]
public class AuthorizationAttribute :
System.Attribute
{
public AuthorizationAttribute(Skill s) {
   Level = s;
}
   public Skill level;
   }
```

Applying attributes to code sections

```
[Authorization(Skill.Senior)]
class CustomerEmployee
{
[Authorization(Skill.Senior)]
public void AssignPrivelege()
{
}
}
```

Inspecting attributes

```
Object[] attrs =
typeof(CustomerEmployee).
GetCustomAttributes(true);
if ((attrs.Length > 0) && (attrs[0] is
AuthorizatioAttribute))
```

```csharp
{
Console.WriteLine("Class [{0}],
accessible by a {1} employee.",
typeof(CustomerEmployee).Name,
((AuthorizatioAttribute)attrs[0]).Level);
}
   MethodInfo[] methodInfos =
   typeof(CustomerEmployee).GetMethods();
foreach (MethodInfo methodInfo in
methodInfos)
{
attrs = methodInfo.GetCustomAttributes
(true);
if ((attrs.Length > 0) && (attrs[0] is
AuthorizatioAttribute))
{
AuthorizatioAttribute a =
(AuthorizatioAttribute)attrs[0];
Console.WriteLine("Method [{0}],
accessible by a {1} employee.",
methodInfo.Name, a.Level);
if(a.Level == Skill.Junior) {
Console.WriteLine("Review, assign prive
section , not accesible by junior
employee");

}
}
    }
```

CHAPTER ELEVEN

Appendix A .NET Types and the Base Object Type

The Mother and root base of all types in .NET is the System.Object type.

Yes!! All .NET types are derived from (inherit) base System.Object type defined in The Framework.

Even the custom types that we define are derived from this base Object class, through inheritance principle we have seen earlier. But, it all happens implicitly without our explicit expression.

To illustrate the point, let's look at some code with regard to the Employee class we defined earlier:

```
 97
 98
 99
100
101
102
103
104             Employee employee = new Employee();
105             Console.WriteLine(employee.ToString());
106
107        }
108
```

The invocation of base Object object's ToString() method

In the above piece of code, in the Console. WriteLine(employee.ToString()) statement, we see, we are invoking the ToString() method, but we didn't define the ToString() method in the Employee class. Then, how come we are able to do that. We are able do that because the Employee class implicitly inherits the Object class defined in the framework. The ToString() method is a member of the Object class and has been inherited by the Employee class implicitly by virtue of inheritance.

The following is the output of the program. What we see in the output is the full name of the class which even includes the namespace the Employee class is part of.

Output:

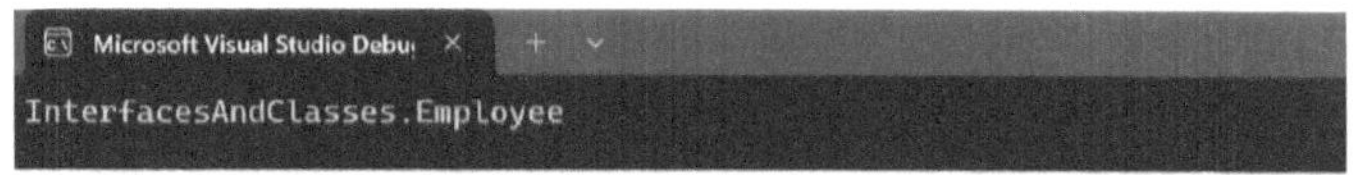

Enter Caption

The other notable methods supported by the Object class are *Equals()*, *GetType()*, *GetHashCode()*.

Type conversions

We can convert one type of object to another provided, the types involved are compatible for conversion.

Going by the Object logic discussed earlier, every other type will be Object type first, and then it is what it is. Like going by what we said earlier, Employee type object is first Object type and then it is Employee type as well.

So that said, we can cast Employee type object, to base Object type. The following makes that clear.

A look at Casting:

```
Object obj = new Employee();
Console.WriteLine(obj.ToString());
```

After running the above code, we still see that the output will be the same as seen above.

The preceding code line is perfectly valid because of the logic we discussed in the previous paragraph. In fact, it would be valid with any other type as well, and not just Employee type.

The base Object type has the ToString() method declared as virtual in it. By virtue of internal default implementation of polymorphism's override feature, we still see the same output as above, for the name of the class.

Boxing and Unboxing

In the above casting example, both types involved are of reference type.

What if one is of reference type and the other value type. That we shall see in the following.

Boxing

Boxing is converting a value type to reference type.

Example code:

```
object i = 100;
```

Now the above variable i, has been assigned the value 100, so it is an integer type. Yes indeed it is **int** type of C#. The real point of discussion now is that **int** is a value type whereas **object** is a reference type. Recalling the point mentioned earlier that value type objects are placed on stack structure in memory and reference types on a heap structure, and for the same reason, something called **boxing** will take place, because of which, value 100 (int object, which is of value type) gets converted to reference type. After int object, 100 has been converted to reference type, int object 100 would be created on heap and then its' reference assigned to i. This is **boxing** a value.

Boxing conversion takes place implicitly.

Unboxing

The opposite of boxing is unboxing, that is, converting a boxed reference type back to its value type is referred to as **Unboxing**. We can unbox what has been boxed. But it **cannot take place implicitly, without explicit casting.** The following code line shows this explicit casting performed in Unboxing.

```
int j = (int) i;
```

CHAPTER TWELVE

Appendix B Reusable, Maintainable, Deployable Code Units

Part - I

Inversion of Control and Dependency Injection Pattern

Before we look at Dependency Injection let us touch upon a software design principle and that is Inversion of Control principle. Inversion of Control is a software design principle that lets avoid direct dependencies between objects. Dependency is when an object depends on another object for its functioning. So let us say, an object A depends on a concrete object B, for it to be functional, then in that case when implementation of this concrete object B changes, object A gets affected. So, there is a direct dependency between objects A and B and they are said to be tightly coupled. **An effective, sound software design of an application is one that offers high cohesion, and, low degree of dependency or loose coupling.**

So that said, one of the factors influencing an effective software design solution of an application is the degree of coupling between dependent objects of an application. So, to have loose coupling, this object B that object A depends on can be defined in terms of an abstract class/interface and thus avoid a direct dependency. This is Inversion of Control.

Dependency Injection pattern is a form of Inversion of Control principle of software design that allows loose coupling and thereby enhances maintainability and testability of application code.

Following is the implementation code example for Constructor based Dependency Injection.

We use the NuGet Package Microsoft.Extensions.Hosting for the implementation. So use the NuGet Package Manager option in Visual Studio to install it.

Constructor based Dependency Injection

```
using System;
using Microsoft.Extensions.Hosting;
using Microsoft.Extensions.
DependencyInjection;

namespace ConsoleApp7
{

    public interface
    IEmpDesignationAuthorityService
```

```
{
    string GetService();
}
public class
EmpManagerAuthorityService :
IEmpDesignationAuthorityService
{
    public string GetService()
    {
        return "Manager service";
    }
}

public class
EmpExecutiveAuthorityService :
IEmpDesignationAuthorityService
{
    public string GetService()
    {
        return "Executive service";
    }
}


public interface
IEmpAuthorityService
{
    void GetService();
}
```

```csharp
public class EmpAuthorityService :
IEmpAuthorityService
    {

        public List<string> EmpAuthority
        Services { get; }

        public EmpAuthorityService
        (IEmpDesignation
        AuthorityService empManager
        AuthorityService)

        {
            EmpAuthorityServices = new
            List<string>()
            {
                empManagerAuthority
                Service.GetService()

            };
        }

        public void GetService()
        {
            foreach (var service in
            EmpAuthorityServices)
            {
                Console.
                WriteLine(service);
```

```csharp
        }
    }

    internal class Program
    {

        static void Main(string[]
        args)
        {
            var host = Host.
            CreateDefaultBuilder()
.ConfigureServices((context,
services) =>
{

            //DI container service
            configuration
            services.AddScoped<IEmp
            DesignationAuthorityService,
            EmpManager
            AuthorityService>();
            services.AddScoped<IEmp
            AuthorityService, Emp
            AuthorityService>(
                serviceProvider => new
                EmpAuthorityService(
                        empManager
                        Authority
                        Service: service
```

```csharp
                        Provider.
                        GetRequired
                        Service
                        <IEmpDesignation
                        Authority
                        Service>()
                )
            );
    })
    .Build();

        var service =
        host.Services.
        GetRequiredService
        <IEmpAuthority
        Service>();
        service.GetService();

        }


            }

    }
}
```

Part - II

.NET terminology that helps us in building reusable, maintainable and deployable units of code

Assembly

An assembly in .NET is an executable code unit of deployment and versioning that stands on its own. An assembly can be representing an application (a .exe file) or it can be a reusable class library (a .dll file).

Class Library

A class library is a reusable bundle of pre-compiled code of classes. One that can be used across applications, because it provides re-usability of code or functions, for addressing a problem of a specific nature or problem domain. For example, when we should work with a set of math functions, and there exists a class library that provides those classes and functions, we simply use it. As and when we see, it serves the purpose and requirements of our application, we use that library. And the good thing is, it is reusable, not just in one application, but across applications.

Package

Microsoft supported mechanism for sharing .NET Code is NuGet.

A **NuGet package** is a single ZIP file that contains code and related files along with a descriptive manifest that includes information like package's version number. Host for a package can be a public host or a private host.

The public host is **nuget.org**, and distribution of the package within an organization can be done through suitable private hosts as well.

In a sum up a NuGet package is nothing but a shareable unit of code.

Part - III

Compilation process of a .NET application

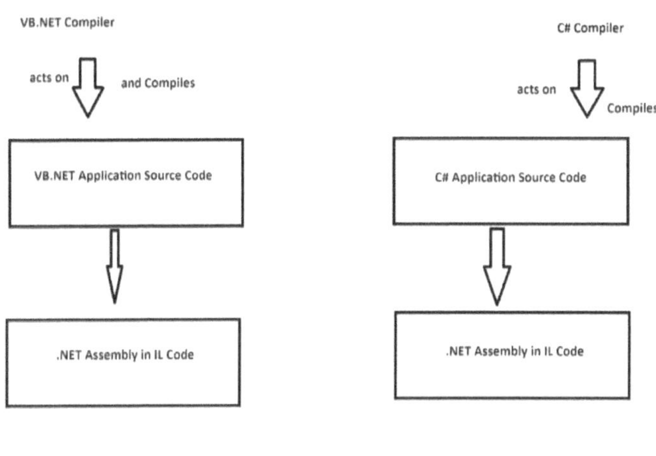

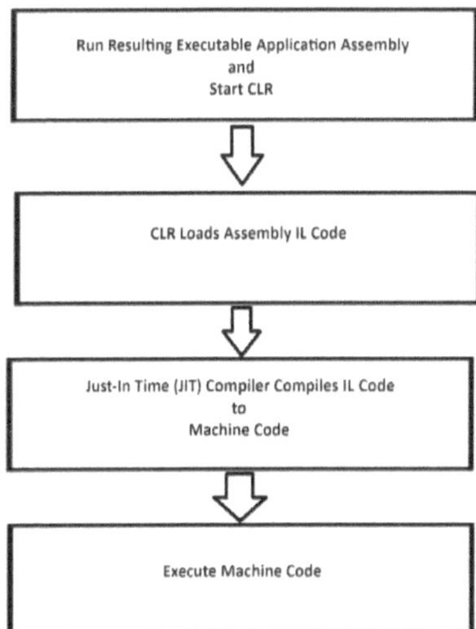

Part - IV

Code Example for Generic EventHandler delegate

```csharp
using System;
using System.Collections.Generic;
using System.Reflection;
using System.Text;


namespace AbcCompany.BusinessObjects
{

    interface IPerson
    {
        void ShowPersonDetails();
    }

    public enum DesignationGroup
    {
        Manager = 0, Executive = 1,
        Assistant = 2, UnAssigned = 3
    }

    public class
    DesignationChangedEventArgs :
    EventArgs
    {
        public readonly DesignationGroup
        LastDesignation, NewDesignation;
```

```csharp
        public DesignationChangedEvent
        Args(DesignationGroup last
        Designation, DesignationGroup
        newDesignation)
        {
            LastDesignation =
            lastDesignation;
            NewDesignation =
            newDesignation;
        }
}


class Employee : IPerson
{
    public Employee() // default
    zero parameter Constructor
    {
        this.Id = "Not set";
        this.Name = "Not set";

    }
    public Employee(string Id,
    string Name) // parameterized
    Constructor
    {
        this.Id = Id;
        this.Name = Name;

    }
```

```csharp
public void ShowPersonDetails()
{
    Console.WriteLine("Emp Id:"
    + Id);
    Console.WriteLine("Emp
    Name:" + Name);
}

public string Id { get; set; }
public string Name { get; set; }
public DesignationGroup
DesignationGroup
{
    get { return
    designationGroup; }
    set
    {
      if (designationGroup ==
      value) return;
      OnDesignationChanged
      (new
      DesignationChangedEventArgs
      (DesignationGroup, value));
        designationGroup =
        value;

    }
}
```

```csharp
    protected virtual void
    OnDesignationChanged(Designation
    ChangedEventArgs e)

    {
        if (DesignationChanged !=
        null)
            DesignationChanged(this, e);
    }

    public event
    EventHandler<DesignationChanged
    EventArgs>? DesignationChanged;

    private DesignationGroup
    designationGroup =
    DesignationGroup.UnAssigned;

}

public class Program
{
    static void Main()
    {

        Employee emp = new
        Employee("Emp200224",
        "Jaban P");
        emp.DesignationChanged +=
        Emp_DesignationChanged;
```

```
        emp.DesignationGroup =
        DesignationGroup.Executive;

        emp.DesignationGroup =
        DesignationGroup.Manager;

    }


    private static void Emp_
    DesignationChanged(object?
    sender,
    DesignationChangedEventArgs e)
    {
        Console.
        WriteLine($"Designation of
        the employee has changed
        from {e.LastDesignation} to
        {e.NewDesignation}");
    }


}


}
```

The book introduces you to C# language and .NET, then object-oriented programming features i.e. **encapsulation, inheritance, polymorphism.** It gradually builds the content on these features in chapters, addressing each of the features in sufficient detail to have a clear grasp of the subject, in harmony with practical, vivid code examples along with listing of the codes. The language used in the book is simple and topics arranged in a logical manner - the key concepts of **classes and objects** that are fundamental to an OOP language are introduced and explained through simple HR application domain parts using Person, Employee objects – such that it appeals to all levels of readers.

Also, the book serves as a refresher as well to those already having some development experience or familiar with the subject, in a new light that may turn out to be interesting.

Author

S. L. Chenoor, has over 15 years of experience in the programming subject, teaching/training fresh graduates and working professionals aspiring to build career in the computer programming field as software developers. He has been a Microsoft Certified Professional in Visual Basic Programming and also holds an MCA degree from a reputed Indian university. He has over a decade of development experience, developing web applications in ASP.NET, PHP and successfully cater to needs of the clients in these environments.

www.ingramcontent.com/pod-product-compliance
Lightning Source LLC
Chambersburg PA
CBHW021215130726

47988CB00002B/673